PRECIOUS PEARLS

Ann Boyce

ARTHUR H. STOCKWELL LTD.
Torrs Park   Ilfracombe   Devon
Established 1898
www.ahstockwell.co.uk

British Library Cataloguing-in-Publication Data.
A catalogue record for this book is available
from the British Library.

ISBN 978-0-7223-3798-1
Printed in Great Britain by
Arthur H. Stockwell Ltd.
Torrs Park   Ilfracombe
Devon

Contents

Easy to Die on a Cross

Some think it was easy to die on a cross –
Just a few nails and some blood loss,
But what about Your torn flesh
As beating after beating they did thresh.
O, the spit, Lord, that stuck to Your beautiful face
Must have made You feel such disgrace.
And, Lord, the walk to Calvary,
Half dead already You were for me.
Remember the thorns twisted to make a crown,
You accepted it, Lord, without a frown.
As the blood poured from Your precious head,
Not a single word You said.
"Yet He opened not His mouth" (*Isaiah 53:7*).
Lord, what about the robe, the laughing and the jeering?
O, and there must have been many who were cheering.
I thank You for all that You had to bear,
Naked and abandoned as You hung there.
Cut off from Your Father, You were for our gain,
You suffered and endured all that pain
To reconcile us to our Father above.
Lord, we cannot fathom Your love.
The sign they nailed above Your head,
Jesus King of the Jews, it said.
Water and blood poured from Your pierced side,
Who'd get Your garments they gambled to decide.
Not one of Your bones were broken,
Scripture fulfilled as it had been spoken.
So You died, Lord, and then You went to the grave;
They even put a huge stone over the cave,
But no stone could hold back God's only Son.
"He's risen, He's risen," were Mary's cries.
She saw Him before He ascended to the skies.
Victory is Yours, Lord,
The battle is won.
At God's right hand in heaven
Sits Jesus, His Son.

Thank You, Lord.

It Is Finished

Jesus came down from heaven to earth
With sinners to dwell,
To teach about the kingdom of heaven
And to warn about hell.
He came as a tiny baby
So that He would be no threat;
He left His crown of glory behind
To come and pay our debt.
He brought hope to those
Who hadn't any
And He came willingly to die,
Not for one, but for many.
No one knew rejection
Better than He,
As He hung naked and abandoned
On Calvary's tree.
The wages of sin is death
And He paid the price for all sin,
With His last breath.
The sins that He took upon Himself were so vast
That they darkened the sky
And the Son of God was cut off
From His Father on high.
He cried out from the Cross at Calvary,
"Father, Father, why hast thou forsaken Me?"
Then with His last breath He cried,
"It is finished." His job was done.
Victory over sin and death was won
On the cross by Jesus, God's only Son.
He willingly died feeling lost and alone,
Because He came to carry out His Father's will
And not His own.
But in the grave He did not stay,
God raised Him up from the dead on the third day.
He ascended to heaven from earth's land
Where He now sits at God's right hand.

Thank You, Lord.

I Have a Dream That Will Not Die

I used to be one of two,
But now I am only one
And sometimes I wonder
If I can get the job done.
Everything I do
I do on my own
And when I drive to new places
I often feel lost and alone.
But I will never give up,
I will continue to try
Because I have a dream
That will not die.
My dream is bigger
Than any fear
And every step I take
Brings it ever near.
I've heard it said that if the dream is big enough
The facts don't count.
Mine is, so I'll push on through
All the problems that mount.
Whether your dream is big or small
Doesn't really matter at all.
The dream is the fuel that you require
To enable you to reach your heart's desire.
So if you used to be one of two
But now you're only one,
Just stay focused on your dream
And you'll get the job done.
It's okay to feel like quitting –
Just don't.
And remember this:
Some will and some won't.
When I've felt like quitting
I've given it one more try,
Because I have a dream
That will not die.

Thank You, Lord.

7

He Came as No Threat

The King of Kings came
As a tiny tot,
And He was laid in a manger,
Not in a fancy cot.
To come as a giant
He was more than able,
But He came as no threat,
Just a little baby born in a stable.
Mary gave birth to
The great I AM,
He had no royal robes to wear
And He had no pram.
This was Father God's plan
That His only Son, Jesus,
Would be born
The Son of man.
There was no doctor present,
Not even a nurse,
Only the stench of the cattle –
What could have been worse?
Why did He come?
You may well ask.
He came to carry out
A very difficult task,
But nothing is impossible
For God's only Son.
He fought the battle against sin and death
And He won.
So as you sing, "Away in a manger
No crib for a bed,"
Remember what John (*3:16*) said:
"For God so loved the world
That He gave His only begotten Son,
That whoever believeth in Him
Should not perish
But have everlasting life."
Hallelujah.

Thank You, Lord.

Transformed

We were all created in God's image,
With clean hands and a pure heart,
But today we are not like
Who we were at the start.
Trials and tribulations
Have left us weary and spent,
With heads bowed low
And backs that are bent.
God is preparing us for the fire that's coming
So we won't be consumed.
Many are willing to be changed,
While some have fumed.
He waits for our permission
To carry out His task
And He won't begin
Unless we ask.
Holy Spirit is changing us
From glory to glory,
And He also enables us to tell
The gospel story.
When a sculptor lets his hammer and chisel fall
On a piece of stone,
Because it's not a living thing
It cannot moan and groan.
But when Holy Spirit carves us up
And cleans us out,
You better believe
That we'll kick, scream and shout.
With each blow of the hammer,
The bad bits get chiselled away,
And only the good bits
Are allowed to stay.
Then after His work
In us is done,
We'll be transformed to look like Jesus,
God's only Son.
Hallelujah.

Thank You, Lord.

God Loves You

No matter where you go or what you do,
Remember this: God loves you.
Whether you're on top of a mountain or in the depths of the sea,
He is right there with you and always will be.
God loves you.
When you talk to Him, that's called prayer,
And He hears every single word that you share.
God loves you.
Even when your face has been beaten to a pulp,
And the pain is so bad that you can barely gulp,
God loves you.
He knows what pain is like.
His only Son, Jesus' face was beaten so bad
That His own mother didn't recognise
The face of her Lad.
Why did Jesus, the Son of God, come down from on high?
Why did He have to suffer and die?
Because God loves you.
But you won't feel God's love unless you accept His Son.
Only then can His will in your life be done.
When we do wrong and say hurtful things,
God calls that sin,
And sin stops God's love from entering in.
The only way He could set us free,
Was to send His Son, Jesus, to die for our sins at Calvary.
Have you ever saved someone that you knew,
And you took the blame for something that you did not do?
That's what Jesus did for you and me;
He took our punishment upon the Cross at Calvary.

Have you ever been punished for stepping out of line?
Did anyone step in to pay your fine?
Jesus did, and He paid the price with the nails,
Yet He opened not His mouth, there were no wails.
He willingly died for you and me,
And the blood that He shed set the captives free,
And all because of love –
A love from our Father in heaven above.
Because Jesus died on the Cross at Calvary,
We are now children of God, adopted into His family,
And through the precious blood that Jesus shed,
We are no longer servants, He calls us sons instead.
God loves you
And there is nothing that we can do to earn it.
It has already been done
On the Cross by Jesus, God's only Son.
Hallelujah.

Thank You, Lord.

His Love Is Not for Sale

Have you ever been so obsessed with something
That you gave God no place?
Have you ever cried to Him for mercy
And He touched you with His grace?
Have you ever been deeply hurt
By someone that you love,
Who you were so close to that you fitted together
Like a hand in a glove?
Have you ever longed for the touch of a loving hand,
Or has the hurt in your heart turned to hatred
Now it's taken command?
Have you ever been abandoned and felt lost and alone,
Because you never knew the love that you should have been shown?
There is a love like no other kind,
That will heal your heart and renew your mind.
"Where can I find it?" you may well say.
It can only be found in Jesus,
He is the Way.
His love will melt away all your sorrow;
His love will give you hope for a brighter tomorrow;
His love will heal all of your pain;
His love will make you whole again;
His love will make you feel great,
So open up your heart and receive it, don't wait.
His love will wash away all your sin,
And when you open the door to your heart, He will pour His love in.

His love is not for sale.
You cannot buy it
His love is free for you and me.
So come now and try it.
You may not know how to ask Him, or what to say;
Maybe you don't know how to pray.
You don't need fancy words,
Just a repentant heart,
And when you ask God to forgive you
For the wrongs you've done, He will,
And He'll give you a brand-new start.
Repentance is turning away from your old ways
Which caused you much pain,
And following God's way
And letting Him reign.
So if you want to feel real cool,
Invite Jesus into your heart
And let Him rule.

Thank You, Lord.

The Choice Is Yours

Why do we end up doing bad things
When we mean to do good?
Why do we not do
The things that we should?
We start out with good intentions,
Then it all turns sour,
And the good we began
Doesn't even last for half an hour.
Have you ever listened to voices
Inside your head,
Telling you to do something
That filled you full of dread?
And when you acted upon
What you were told,
Did you not realise that you were being controlled?
There are two choices you can make –
Which one will it be?
Will you choose to be under the spirit of control
Or the one who will set you free?
Two choices –
One good, one bad.
One will make you happy, and the other will make you sad.
Two choices –
One will set you free, the other will bind you up in chains.
Two choices –
One is right, the other is wrong.
Two choices –
Will you choose to win, or will you choose to lose?
Two choices –
One leads to life, the other to death.
Choose life while you still have breath.
Jesus is the Way, the Truth and the Life –
Choose Him today
And He will deliver you from all strife.
The choice is yours.

Thank You, Lord.

Praise God

These poems may convict you,
But they will not condemn.
If you agree, praise God
With a loud amen.
The words are from God, they are not my own,
I just write down what He says,
And with every stroke of the pen
I give Him the praise.
He gave them to me,
To give to you,
And what He gives
Is pure and true.
"Every good gift and every perfect gift
Is from above" (*James 1:17*),
And I thank God for this wonderful gift
Which I truly love.
I am so eager to hear
What He has to say,
So I quietly listen to Him
Day after day.
If your heart is touched
By what I write,
That will be thanks enough for me
If that's all right.
Though I am the one
Who tells the story,
It's my Lord God who is worthy
Of all the glory.
Hallelujah.

Thank You, Lord.

God Is Melting My Heart

In days gone by
I never used to cry,
But somehow today
I'm constantly wiping the tears away,
But, hallelujah,
God is melting my heart.
It must have been like an iceberg,
So hard to part.
He doesn't chip at it with an ice pick,
That is not His way.
He just pours in His love
And all the ice melts away.
So if your tears
Just won't stop dripping,
Praise God for all the ice
That He is stripping.
And after there has been
A mighty flood,
Your heart will be cleansed
Of all the mud.
So don't dam up your tears,
Allow them to flow,
And instead of having a heart of ice,
You'll have one as white as the snow.

Thank You, Lord.

Walk in Faith and Victory

Out with the old, in with the new –
I have something greater planned for you.
Trust in Me day by day,
I will show you where to go and what to say.
Put on your cloak of willingness,
And I will cover you in the robe of righteousness.
Go spread My greatest commandments
Throughout the land.
Keep it simple so people
Will understand.
"Thy word is a lamp unto my feet,
And a light unto my path"(*Psalm 119:105*).
Walk in faith and victory
And you won't know defeat.
Without vision, man will perish,
And doubt will hold you back from all that you cherish.
Clean the slate, don't you wait,
Changing your thinking will open the gate.
Fill your mind with positive affirmation,
Then boldly go out and touch the nation.
When you give away the love that I give,
My love will change how people think and live.
I only give to those who ask,
And when you do I will equip you to do the task.
Go boldly where you've not gone before;
Fear not, for I will be ahead of you, opening up the door.
"And you shall love the Lord your God with all your heart,
With all your soul, and with all your mind, and with all your strength."
This is the first commandment and the second like it is this:
"You shall love your neighbour as yourself."
There is no other commandment greater than these
And you can read them in Mark 12:30 and 31 if you please.

Thank You, Lord.

Memories

When we take a trip down memory lane
We remember the things that caused us great pain.
We also encounter fond memories that are good
And they make us happy, just as they should.
We remember, too, yesterday's hopes and fears,
And when we think about what was
We're sure to shed a few tears.
Our minds are like banks, never holding the same amount,
And if there were no memories to withdraw
We'd have to close our account.
Sometimes, as we take a stroll down memory lane,
We come across locked doors that keep in the pain.
We remember it all, but we just walk on by,
Because the hurts that are hidden would cause us to cry.
Everything that we do or say gets deposited in our minds
To withdraw one day.
The good and the bad go in without a doubt,
And whatever goes in will surely come out.
If we don't deal with our past, it'll hold us enslaved,
And we won't walk into the future
For which we've been saved.
Past fears will certainly hold you back
From an incredible future where there is no lack.
Face up to your fears and let Jesus unlock the door,
Then your fears will be gone for evermore.
He has the key to unlock every door to your heart,
But He won't open any until you ask Him to start.
And once you have given Him free reign,
Your sad memories will never haunt you again.
"If the Son therefore shall make you free,
Ye shall be free indeed" (*John 8:36*).
Hallelujah.

Thank You, Lord.

18

Lift Your Vision Higher

God has buried your sins
In an ocean so vast,
But some of you keep on
Digging up the past.
When you dig up things that have been buried
But not forgotten,
They are sure to bring decay
Because they are rotten.
The former things have taken place,
It's time to close the old doors,
Open up the new,
And go win the race.
Yesterday has gone
With all of its pain,
But if you keep on talking about it
You'll resurrect it again.
When you're always looking back,
You won't see what's in front,
And without clear vision
You're sure to have a dunt.
Lift your vision higher than ever before,
And go for God's best,
Which is so much more.
"Be ye transformed by the renewing of your mind" (*Romans 12:2*).
Just empty out all the negative thoughts
And fill it with the positive kind.
Lay down your heavy load at the foot of the Cross
And the Lord, your God, will burn up all the dross.
Lay it down, then walk away.
Jesus said, "Trust in Me, I am the Way" (*John 14:6*).

Thank You, Lord.

His Banqueting Table

We fill our bodies
With all sorts of stuff,
And there are times when we simply
Can't get enough.
We eat so much
That we soon start to swell,
And when we look in the mirror
Our reflection will tell.
We become so obsessed with food
That we forget about God.
It's no wonder we get out of shape
And look a bit odd.
When we try to diet
Our cravings seem to grow,
Then we eat in secret
So no one will know.
We even hide the sweetie papers
Way down in the bin,
And we nearly choke on the chocolate
When someone unexpectedly walks in.
After we've eaten something
That we said we would not,
We deny it and feel ashamed
Because we got caught.
But there is a food that is good,
That won't cause a weight gain,
And it will heal our hearts
And take away our pain.
Jesus has prepared for us
A banqueting table,
And when we eat of the Bread of Life (*John 6:35*)
He will make us more than able.
So instead of stuffing our bodies
With junk food galore,
Let's come to the Lord's table
And receive so much more.

Thank You, Lord.

Trust in the Lord

If you want to find calm waters
In stormy seas,
Your place of safety
Is on your knees.
It's in your humility
That you'll find great release.
Trust in the Lord, your God,
The Prince of Peace.
When the winds of adversity
Come to overwhelm,
Focus on Me, I am at the helm.
I will steer your course
Throughout the land,
I will uphold you
With My righteous right hand (*Isaiah 41:10*).
Fear not for I am with you,
Do not be dismayed,
I will answer the prayers
That you have prayed.
I will enable you to leave this familiar shore
And take you to places you've never been before.
I will equip you for the task, and all you have to do is ask.
If you don't act on what I have said,
Your hopes and dreams will all lie dead.
But if you dare to heed the call,
You'll get more than a little – you'll receive it all.
I am Jehovah Jireh, the God who provides.
Don't take baby steps, take great big strides.
"Trust in the Lord with all your heart,
And lean not on your own understanding" (*Proverbs 3:5*).
"In all your ways acknowledge Him
And He will make straight your paths" (*Proverbs 3:6*).

Thank You, Lord.

The Power of Prayer

When things go wrong I often hide away,
But God has told me that is not His way.
We must not keep anything concealed
Cos it's through the power of prayer
That we get healed.
We are all part of one body, and we need one another,
So it's good to reveal our hurts to a sister or brother.
There is power in the prayer of two
Cos Jesus said,
"Where two or three are gathered together in My name,
There am I in the midst of them" (*Matthew 18:20*).
So if more than one brings Jesus' power,
I'll not even hide for half an hour.
I will run to the phone and ask for help,
And no more will I sit at home and yelp.
God's ways are not our ways,
But we must obey what He says.
This is what I've learned today:
That if I hide away, no one will pray.
But if I bring the pain into God's light,
He is faithful and just to make things right.
I am not truly God-dependent
If I'm not also dependent on the body of Christ.
Please forgive me.
I need you and I love you.
If we let something niggle away at us
That's just the size of a gnat,
Very soon that tiny little thing
Will become bigger than a bat.
Don't make a mountain out of a molehill,
"Be still and know that I am God" (*Psalm 46:10*).
You have made the enemy a giant,
When he is only a gnat.
But you have the power within to swat him away,
So lift up your bat.
"Submit yourselves therefore to God,
Resist the devil,
And he will flee from you" (*James 4:7*).

Thank You, Lord.

His Provision

People seem to be rushing
Here there and everywhere,
Buying lots of things
That they'll never wear.
Because it's a bargain,
They rush to buy with great haste,
And they don't care about the size
Or whether it's their taste –
What a waste!
They spend all of their money,
With none left to spare,
And when they go home for a bite to eat
The cupboard is bare.
What they earned in a month,
In one day is all spent.
Now their heads are bowed low
And their backs are bent.
When will they ever learn
Not to spend all that they earn?
Once we've become better stewards
Of what we've been given,
We'll receive much more
From our Father in heaven.
Whatever God gives
To His creation
Is His provision
To feed the nation.
Though we may have plenty,
We should spend with great care
Then there will always be enough left
To go out and share.
Whatever we give away,
So we've been told,
Will always come back
One hundredfold.

Thank You, Lord.

My God Is an Awesome God

In the midst of the storm
My God was there,
And when I cried out to Him
He heard my prayer.
He walked beside me
Through the valley of pain,
And because He was with me
The pain did not reign.
Though it hurt so much,
I knew His peace,
And because I trusted in Him,
I knew the pain would cease.
Though I did not get
Instant relief,
This challenge has certainly
Strengthened my belief.
God's promises are for ever true.
His word says,
"I will never leave you or forsake you" (*Hebrews 13:5*).
"Though sorrow may last for a night,
Joy comes in the morning" (*Psalm 30:5*),
And I thank God
For the new day that's dawning.
I praise God for the pain
Which showed that something was wrong,
And now it's been revealed,
He will make me strong.
My God is an awesome God,
Who really does care about me,
And wherever I am
There He will be.

Thank You, Lord.

Say a Prayer

When you are in pain
And in the depths of despair,
It's so good to hear the voices
Of people who care.
When a friend phones you
To say a prayer,
You can actually feel love and encouragement
Flowing over the air.
I thank God for giving me
Ears to hear,
So that I can listen to words
That bring hope and good cheer.
There are times when we cannot
Meet together,
Maybe through illness
Or just the bad weather.
If you start to feel uplifted
Out of the blue,
You can be sure that someone
Is praying for you.
If Jesus, the Son of God,
Needed to pray,
Then so do we
Every single day.

Thank You, Lord.

Thank You, Lord

Lord, you are my Saviour
And the One who protects,
And when I sail stormy waters
Your light projects.
Instead of hitting the rocks
Your guidance steers me clear.
Thank You, Lord, that You
Are for ever near.
When fear overwhelms me,
And I cry out in fright,
You are my beacon burning
Throughout the night.
You are my pillar of strength when I am weak.
Lord, help me to listen more whenever You speak.
When I am in danger of being bitten by the shark,
Lord, You are my hope in the dark.
You are faithful when all else fails.
Lord, You are the wind beneath my sails.
There is no God besides You,
Nor any other Rock (*Isaiah 44:8*).
Thank You, Lord, for choosing me
To be one of Your flock.
Thank You for forgiving me
For the sins of the past.
You alone, Lord, are the First and the Last (*Isaiah 44:6*).

Thank You for all the good gifts
That You have given,
And for teaching me to be a better steward
Of Your provision.
Thank You for changing me to be like Your Son,
So that You may use me on earth,
Your will to be done.
Thank You for Your sufficient grace
To bear life's ails.
Thank You, Lord, for suffering
The pain of the nails.
Thank You for the Cross
Where You died for me.
Thank You, Lord, for setting me free.
And as it was said,
So let it be,
That I would love others
The way You love me.

Thank You, Lord.

Focus on the Prize

We all have a God-given destiny
Placed within our heart,
And nothing or no one
Can make it depart.
What God has given to us
He will never take back,
And through Him we have the ability
To go and fill up our sack.
It's up to us
What choices we make,
So we shouldn't blame anyone else
When we make a mistake.
The path least walked upon
May cause some stress,
But it's a small price to pay
For the joy of success.
When opportunity knocks
Be quick to open the door,
And step out in faith
To where you've not gone before.
You may feel uncomfortable
Being out of your comfort zone,
But rest assured that you will not walk alone.
What you see as a mountain
Is just a molehill in disguise,
So take your eyes off the obstacles
And focus on the prize.
The ladder is in place
And now is the time,
Enjoy the journey
As you start to climb.
You may not have to put your foot on every rung
To get to the top;
You might find yourself taking
A jump, skip and a hop.
Once you've got momentum going
You must not stop,
And before you know it
You'll have reached the top.

Thank You, Lord.

Come to Me

When the road that you're travelling
Seems to be all uphill,
It's good to take a little rest
And just be still.
In the quiet times
You will know God's peace,
Then all of your aches and pains
Will surely cease.
Rest refreshes the body,
Heart and soul.
It also restores the energy you need
To reach the next goal.
In this fast-paced world
People are running to and fro,
And some have forgotten how to relax
And don't know how to go slow.
Jesus said, "Come to Me, all you who labour
And are heavy laden,
And I will give you rest" (*Matthew 11:28*).
"Take My yoke upon you,
And learn from Me,
For I am gentle and lowly in heart
And you will find rest for your souls" (*Matthew 11:29*).
"For My yoke is easy
And My burden is light" (*Matthew 11:30*).
So, as you are running
Here, there and everywhere,
Remember the yoke that you wear
Determines the burden you bear.

Thank You, Lord.

Stand up, Little Children

Stand up, little children, and take your place,
For you are the future of the human race.
I know what it's like to be a child in an adult world,
But now it's time to get your banner of hope unfurled.
You live in a world where there is so much chaos,
With nation fighting against nation
Cos they both want to be the boss.
Stand up, little children, and obey My command:
Go and spread the good news throughout the land.
Listen, children, one and all,
When you hear God's voice, pay attention to the call.
God called to Samuel as he lay asleep on his bed,
But he didn't know it was God,
So he went to his master, Eli, instead.
Samuel must have thought Eli was a bit odd
When after the third call he said it was God.
Can you imagine the look on that young boy's face
When he was called by the Saviour of the human race?
He must have wondered why God called his name,
But, saved or unsaved, He can use us all the same.
So if you should wake up in the middle of the night, do not fear,
Cos Jesus, your Saviour, is ever near (*Hebrews 13:5*).
He neither slumbers nor sleeps
As over you a watchful eye He keeps.
God will call whoever He chooses,
So be ready to listen when He interrupts your snoozes.
We should thank God, for giving us a mouth and two ears,
So when He calls us we can say,
"Speak, Lord, your servant hears" (*1 Samuel 3:10*).

If we are willing, God will make us able,
And He has invited everyone to come and eat at His table.
God chose Samuel to get a message
From Himself to Eli,
And He once chose a donkey,
So why not you and I?
If you want to see and hear more,
Just say yes when I call.
Then bit by bit
I will reveal it all.
Jesus said, "Let the little children come to Me
And forbid them not,
For of such is the kingdom of God"(*Mark 10:14*).

Thank You, Lord.

New Fruit

God, You are so big
And I am so small,
Yet You know everything about me;
You alone know it all.
Your power and Your majesty
Blow my mind.
There is no one else like You
In all of mankind.
You know every single hair
On my head,
And You resurrected my hopes and dreams
That once lay dead.
Your creation is a wonder
To behold,
And one touch of Your hand
Makes me bold.
The seasons come
And the seasons go,
But there is one thing
That I surely know.
No matter where I am,
There You will be.
Your word says that You'll never
Leave or forsake me (*Hebrews 13:5*).
Although today
The trees are bare,
Before very long
New fruit will be there.
The seeds that were planted
Have taken root,
And when the time is right
They will start to shoot.
Then those little seeds
That you thought were dead
Will bring forth an abundant harvest
So that you all can be fed.

Thank You, Lord.

The Grace of God

Lord, no matter what adversity
I have had to face,
My life is living proof
Of Your mercy and grace.
When I fell down
You lifted me back up,
And when I was thirsty You gave me
A drink from Your cup.
When I struggled with many burdens
Along life's road,
You helped me to carry
My heavy load.
Even in the darkness,
Where I hid in disgrace,
Your light shone upon
My tear-stained face.
You forgave me
For all the things I did wrong,
And in my weakness
You are made strong.
You died on the Cross
To set me free,
And You buried my sins
In the deepest sea.
Today when I see alcohol abuse
And hear of drugs that make people high,
I remember there but for the grace of God
Go I.

Thank You, Lord.

Trust in the Lord

Have you ever sat in a hospital waiting room
Not knowing what you were going to hear?
Has your heart ever pounded so hard
Because it was full of fear?
But once the truth was brought out
Into the light
You actually felt some relief
And began to feel all right.
Where there are challenges,
There fear and worry are bound to be.
Remember God's word said,
"You shall know the truth, and the truth shall set you free" (*John 8:32*).
No one but God knows what tomorrow will bring,
So for today let's stand together in unity and sing.
Praise the Lord with all your heart,
And your sea of misery He will part.
God said that we should praise Him in every situation,
So let's open the doors of praise and let the Lord in
To heal His creation.
Rejoice whether the news is good or bad,
Then you'll soon be having more fun than you've ever had.
Laughter brings healing upon its wings,
It holds the cure for many things.
Proverbs 17 verse 22 has these words written within:
"A merry heart does good like a medicine."
So whatever you hear from hospital staff,
In the face of adversity stand up and laugh.
Laughter will blow all the dark clouds away;
Laughter is a tonic, so drink some today.
Remember that God is a God who cares
And He can rescue you from the devil's snares.

God is faithful and He is ever near.
You will know His peace when you trust in Him
To take away your fear.
"Trust in the Lord with all your heart
And lean not on your own understanding" (*Proverbs 3:5*).
"In all your ways
Acknowledge Him,
And He shall direct your paths" (*Proverbs 3:6*).
Man may find a cure,
But it is God who heals,
So we must trust in God and not in man,
No matter the hand life deals.

Thank You, Lord.

God Is Faithful

God will lift your head up high,
He will also comfort you whenever you cry.
God alone will make your paths straight,
He is always on time and is never ever late.
He will hold your hand
When you're weary and spent,
He will straighten you up
When your back is bent.
God is faithful (*1 Corinthians 10:13*)
And He will see you through.
He promised never to leave
Or forsake you (*Hebrews 13:5*).
He will give you strength
When you have none,
And He'll help you to fight the battles
That need to be won.
God sees the end from the beginning,
And when you trust in Him you'll soon be winning.
He knows your pain and how bad it feels.
God is Jehovah Rapha, the God who heals.
He is your Heavenly Father
And this is what He wants you to do:
1 Peter 5:7 says, "Casting all your care upon Him,
For He cares for you."
"Trust in the Lord with all your heart" (*Proverbs 3:5*)
And your sea of misery He will part.
Though you're in the midst of a storm do not fear,
Jesus, your Saviour, is ever near.
"I sought the Lord,
And He heard me,
And delivered me
From all my fears" (*Psalm 34:4*).
"This poor man cried,
And the Lord heard him,
And saved him out of all his troubles" (*Psalm 34:6*).

Thank You, Lord.

God Was There

When my husband became ill
And I found it hard to be still,
God was there.
When the going got tough
And I felt a bit rough,
God was there.
When I lay awake at night
And could barely see the light,
God was there.
When I needed a miracle to see me through
And as I struggled to do what I had to do,
God was there.
When the pain became more than I could bear
And I cried out to God in prayer,
God was there.
When my loved one died and I was left on my own,
I never once felt lost and alone,
God was there.
When the days turned to months and the months to years,
And I cried and cried so many tears,
God was there.
When I look back now I remember with joy
All the good times I had with my Danny Boy,
And even now as I wipe away a tear
I know that God is ever near.
God is faithful (*1 Corinthians 10:13*)
And His promises true.
He said, "I will never leave you or forsake you" (*Hebrews 13:5*).
God has a great future planned for me (*Jeremiah 29:11*),
And nothing or no one will keep it from coming to be –
No height, depth, breadth or length,
Because the joy of the Lord is my strength (*Nehemiah 8:10*).
It is only by God's grace that I am standing in this place.
You see, I lost the love of my life.
His name was Danny and I was his wife.
Now today I can say,
"I can do all things
Through Christ which strengthens me" (*Philippians 4:13*).

Thank You, Lord.

Change

When we plant a seed
It won't bloom in half an hour.
It takes time to grow into
A beautiful flower.
To produce a harvest
Is that little seed's aim,
But without change
Things will remain the same.
From big seeds to little seeds
To seeds of all ranges,
If nothing changes,
Nothing changes.
So when you plant your crop
You will have to wait
And at the right time the harvest will be ready,
Never early or late.
People also need
Time to grow.
Some will grow fast
While others grow slow.
It's in the struggle
That your true colours will show,
And it's in the soil of adversity
That the best fruit will grow.

Thank You, Lord.

Together, Together

Forget about all the problems that have mounted,
It's time for us to stand up and be counted.
There are giants that we all have to face,
Every single one of us in the human race.
But we have the choice
To lift up our voice
And say to them,
"Off with your head!"
Then the giants that we feared
Will soon lie dead.
When we face up to our fear,
It's courage that will make it disappear.
The ones who stand fast, though their bones may rattle,
Are the ones who'll have the victory in every battle.
There are battles going on all around us,
Though we may not be aware,
And it's up to us to overcome them if we dare.
He who dares wins.
It would be foolish to try to go it alone,
But when we're part of the team
No one will be on their own.
No man is an island, so we should join with the team,
Then together each one can achieve his dream.
No wars were ever won by one;
Only when we march together in unity
Will the battle be won.
So it's time to arise
And go claim your prize.
With swords at the ready and the shield in your hand,
It's time now to go and take the land.
March together as a solid block
And focus on Me.
I am the Rock.
Unity is a mighty weapon to hold in your hand,
And when you're together, together
I will give you the land.
An army divided against itself will fall,
So bind yourselves together in love,
Then you'll receive it all.

Thank You, Lord.

But He Could Not Be Hidden

We put God in a box and say,
"There, there, just You stay in there.
If I need Your help
I'll call You in prayer."
We think that we can do
All things by ourselves,
So we put God in His box
At the back of the dusty shelves.
We open up the little box once in a while,
And wonder why God never seems to smile.
Then we close the lid and store the little box away,
And if we should need Him we might let Him out one day.
There are no containers big enough to hold God,
Though they may have really strong locks.
God cannot and will not
Be contained in any box.
"But He could not be hid" (*Mark 7:24*).
Perhaps we put Him in the little box
Because we think that we are greater,
But nothing or no one is greater
Than God, our creator.
The higher we think we are, the lower we will fall.
God's word reveals it all.
He said that pride always comes before a fall (*Proverbs 16:18*),
And when we do we won't be walking quite so tall.
As well as putting God in a box,
We box ourselves in
And we hide away
Because we're ashamed of our sin.
But God's ways are not our ways.
He doesn't want our sins to be concealed,
Because that which is not revealed
Cannot be healed.
We have a choice whether to reveal or conceal,
And when we get real, God can heal.
Break open all the boxes
That you have built,
And the Lord, your God,
Will wash away all the silt.

Thank You, Lord.

You Are Fearfully and Wonderfully Made

I used to put a mask on
For every occasion,
But I didn't realise
I was hiding God's creation.
I thought that everyone else
Was better than me,
So I hid who God
Had created me to be.
At times my mask would slip
And the real me would show,
Then in fear of being criticised
Back behind my mask I would go.
God has taught me not to take offence
At what someone has said,
And that I should dwell on
His healing word instead.
God said, "You are fearfully
And wonderfully made" (*Psalm 139:14*).
These words bring me
Great joy and peace,
And never again will I mask
God's masterpiece.

Thank You, Lord.

Hugs of Love

My father and my mother both did their very best,
But I missed them holding me next to their breast.
Although they worked very hard to provide,
What I needed the most always seemed to hide.
There was never any lack of clothes for my back,
And the home-made food for my tummy was very yummy,
But I missed out on the hugs of love from my daddy and mummy.
I was criticised more than I was praised,
And that's the way my brothers, sisters and I were raised.
Some children were told not to play with me,
And I often wondered what the reason could be.
Was it because I came from a large family?
Encouragement mostly came from outside the family house,
And these words made me feel like a giant
Instead of a mouse.
When we are deprived of loving hugs in our childhood,
We grow up not feeling as loved as we should.
Though I felt rejected, I still loved my parents,
I can honestly say,
And by God's grace I bear no grudges against them today.
It must have been the norm, way back in those days,
For parents not to hug their children or give them much praise.
Perhaps they thought that love and praise
Would spoil their child,
But I believe the lack of it can make them wild.
I thank God for my parents, who did the best that they could,
And I love and respect their memory
Just as God said that I should.
We cannot give what we have not got,
But when we ask God for more of His love, He will give us a lot.

God said "You do not have because you do not ask" (*James 4:2*).
"Ask and it shall be given" (*Matthew 7:7*).
I once met a man called Charlie Jones,
Who hugged every man with glee,
But he politely kissed the back of the ladies' hands –
That was his way, you see.
One day he received a letter from a man he had hugged,
And this is what he said:
'Up until now no one has ever hugged me,
And the day that you hugged me I was seventy-three!'
Whether you are three, seventy-three or one hundred and three,
If you would like a hug,
Come and get one from me.

Thank You, Lord.

You Are the God of Miracles

Lord, You know my needs before I ask,
And when I do You give me what I need to complete my task.
In the dead of night You hear my prayer.
What a comfort to know, Lord, that You are there!
Jesus, Your name is above every other name,
And since I came to know You, I have never been the same.
You are the God of miracles,
And You can do what others cannot do,
O, my Lord and my Saviour, how I really need You.
When I'm climbing a mountain, You are there,
And Your love even covers me in the depths of despair.
When I'm weary and faltering along life's road,
You help me to carry my heavy load.
You are mighty and awesome and wonderful to behold,
And Your love is more precious to me than silver or gold.
Open the eyes of my heart so that I might see
The wonderful future You've got planned for me.
Lord, will You give me a glimpse of Your beautiful face?
And will You touch me with Your mercy and grace?
One touch of Your hand makes me so bold,
And Your love melts my heart when it's icy and cold.
There are so many things I don't understand,
But I know that You hold me in the palm of Your hand.
When my boat gets rocked, You give me peace,
And when I hold on to You, all my wanderings cease.
When my spirit is heavy, I do what Your word says:
I rise up and put on the garment of praise (*Isaiah 61:3*).
Whether my situation is good or bad,
When I praise You and not the problem
It's You that makes me glad.
You have turned for me my mourning into dancing (*Psalm 30:11*)
And my sorrow into joy.
Thank You for helping me to live without my Danny Boy.
"I can do all things
Through Christ which strengthens me" (*Philippians 4:13*).

Thank You, Lord.

A Good Leader

A good leader is always a step ahead of the pack,
And he leads from the front and not from the back.
A good leader encourages others to do their best,
And he knows that being bossy puts friendships to the test.
A good leader always gives his team time to grow,
And he knows that some will grow fast, while others will grow slow.
A good leader is patient and knows how to affirm,
He avoids using words that make people squirm.
A good leader is gentle and lowly in heart,
And his love for others sets him apart.
A good leader lifts you up when you're feeling down,
And his encouraging words will wash away your frown.
A good leader knows the dangers of taking offence,
He teaches against what will breach your defence.
A good leader guides you in the paths that are good,
And he cares for you, just as he said he would.
A good leader shares his success with others,
And he's always willing to help his sisters and brothers.
A good leader will listen and feel your pain,
And he will walk with you through the wind and the rain.
Who is your leader?
Choose whom you follow with great care.
My leader is Jesus, and He promised
That He'd always be there.
He loves with an everlasting love,
And His unconditional love comes from
His Father above.
He is the King of Kings,
Who sits on the throne,
And He is the greatest leader
The world has ever known.

Thank You, Lord.

Jesus Came to Set Us Free

Have you ever been controlled
By a family member or a friend,
But you were too afraid to speak up
In case your friendship would end?
Were you too busy rationalising
To realise that your peace had been destroyed,
And that you were no longer happy
Because you were feeling annoyed?
Some people don't know that they're being controlling,
And if you don't tell them,
They'll keep on rocking and rolling.
We were born to soar, not to settle,
So we must rise above words that would sting us
Like a jaggy nettle.
Fear makes us cling,
Faith enables us to let go.
When we trust in God with all of our heart,
His peace we will know.
If we allow man to control us,
We'll never become who God intended us to be.
Satan uses people to bind us,
Jesus came to set us free.
Proverbs 29:25 says, "The fear of man brings a snare,
But whoever puts his trust in the Lord will be safe."
Speaking the truth in love
Will loose the shackles that held you bound,
But when you confront the spirit of control,
Offence will often be found.

The very thing that held you back from speaking out,
Is now threatening you
With its very loud shout.
"I am offended," offence will say,
But when you stand up to it,
It will soon run away.
James 4:7 says, "Submit yourselves therefore to God,
Resist the devil, and he will flee from you."
If someone takes offence when the truth has been spoken
It is not your fault,
So do not let them drag you down
By their verbal assault.
Jesus said, "You shall know the Truth,
And the Truth shall make you free" (*John 8:32*).

Thank You, Lord.

Let's Raise Our Praise

Whenever you feel the blow of the enemy's skelp,
Do not sit at home and yelp.
Fix your eyes on me; I am your help.
If you stay focused on the problem, it will not cease,
And a mind in turmoil won't know any peace.
If you don't put fuel on a fire, it will soon go out,
But if you keep on fanning the flame, up it will sprout.
Attacks will come, have no doubt, and when they do, give Me a shout.
I will hear you loud and clear. I am your Saviour and I am ever near.
You have two choices, which one will it be?
You can either focus on the problem or fix your eyes on Me.
The problem won't always instantly cease,
But I will be with you and you will know My peace.
And out of the struggle where you wrestled with doom and gloom,
You will emerge changed and more beautiful
Than a rose in full bloom.
It's in the struggle that your character is built.
Walk through it with Me and I'll wash away all the silt.
You may think that your struggle has gone on for too long,
But it's in the struggle that you are made strong.
Welcome each struggle and praise Me in every one,
Then I will enable you to get the job done.
Praise Me in all situations, whether good or bad.
When you praise Me, I will make you joyful and glad.
Praising Me puts Me on the throne,
And when you praise Me you will never walk alone.
Praise Me and I will send My power,
And I will make you into a strong tower.
It's in the praises of My people that I dwell.
Praise Me and I will rescue you from the gates of hell.
Praise the Lord wherever you are,
Whether you're washing the dishes or driving your car.
So let's raise our praise to the God of Creation,
Then wait on Him to heal every nation.
Do not listen to the whispers in your ear,
Because Satan is a liar,
And God told me that very soon
His pants would be on fire.
Hallelujah.

Thank You, Lord.

Praise God

Lord, since I came to know You,
I have never been the same.
Now I am living day by day
In the glory of Your name.
I will not move,
Unless You tell me to,
Because I can do nothing
Without help from You.
But, "I can do all things
Through Christ which strengthens me" (*Philippians 4:13*).
Just when I think
That I'm getting there,
I always seem to end up
In a pit of despair.
I have come to realise
That when I'm almost touching the prize
The obstacles seem to become
A much greater size.
But I've noticed that if I
Keep on pushing through,
The path of adversity leads to
A better view.
The struggle is nothing
Compared to the reward,
So I'll stop looking back,
And I'll keep moving forward.
When you are about to reach the summit
Don't look down or else you'll plummet.
Climb over the boulders that try to block,
And keep your feet firmly planted
Upon the Rock.
Praise God with every step that you take,
And you'll have the victory, make no mistake.
Rest a little while at the pit stops that are there,
But you'll get stuck if you sit too long
In your comfortable chair.

Thank You, Lord.

Sin No More

Please don't think that I'm perfect,
Because I am not.
I'm a sinner like you,
Just in case you forgot.
But God is changing me,
Day by day,
And when He has taken out all the bad bits
I'll be like Jesus one day.
God could do the job
So much quicker,
But I've allowed my sins to stick
Like a great big sticker.
Every time I ask Him to peel them off,
I'm ashamed and cry out, "No!"
So my sins stay stuck in the mud,
Where they'll multiply and grow.
But when I'm ready to repent
Of what I've done wrong,
He'll welcome me back into His arms
Where I belong.
Then He will take His axe
To the root of my sin,
And cut them off, so that none
Will stay hidden within.
Then my Father
Will whisper to me,
"You are forgiven,
And your sins are buried in the deepest sea."
Then I'll hear Him say,
As I've heard before,
"Now go, My child,
And sin no more" (*John 5:14*).

Thank You, Lord.

Bouquet of Praise

Each one of us is different,
And we all bear some scars,
But we often try to hide these grey dots,
By covering them up with stars.
God wants us to be real,
And not to pretend,
Then whatever we reveal
He will surely mend.
God thinks we are more precious
Than silver or gold,
And what he has in store for us
Will bring joy untold.
So let's raise our bouquet of praise
Above all the hurtful things,
And offer it as a sweet aroma
To the King of Kings.
Hallelujah.

Thank You, Lord.

Good and Bad

Good and bad are opposites;
One is black and the other is white.
Good will always stand up to bad
When he comes looking for a fight.
Good will stand his ground
In the midst of a battle;
Bad tries to fill good full of fear
So that his bones will rattle.
Good says words that bring health to the body,
Just like good food;
Bad will make you feel ill
With words that are no good.
Good loves at all times,
His love is from above;
Bad is so full of hatred
That he can't show any love.
Good always builds people up,
He knows how to edify;
Bad loves to tear you down,
And he knows how to make you cry.
Good and bad battle it out in our minds
Each and every day,
But the choice is ours to kick one out
And let the other one stay.
Bad will dissolve
When we change our thinking,
And when we fill our minds with good thoughts,
It will no longer be stinking.
I'm gonna wash the bad right out of my mind,
I'm gonna wash the bad right out of my mind,
I'm gonna wash the bad right out of my mind,
And send him on his way.
"Be transformed by the renewing of your mind" (*Romans 12:2*).

Thank You, Lord.

The Pen Is Mightier Than the Sword

When is the pen mightier
Than the sword?
When you use it,
Thus says the Lord.
So use it well,
And write what I tell,
Then in the land of milk and honey
You will dwell.
Share these words,
Near and far,
Push wide the door
That's been held ajar.
Stay focused on Me
In all that you do,
And go take the land
That I promised to you.
There is much, much more
In store –
So much
That you will soar.
Step out in faith
With the pen in your hand,
And go spread the Good News
Throughout the land.
Do not look
To the left or right,
And write the words down
That I tell you to write.
Do not be afraid
Of territories unknown,
Because I will be with you,
You will not walk alone.

Thank You, Lord.

Peace from Within

Peace from within
Will get you through what's without,
So be of good cheer
When the storms come about.
Hold on to the Rock,
Upon which you stand,
Then go forth and preach the Good News
Throughout all the land.
It's time to get your banner
Of hope unfurled,
And wave it over
This hurting world.
Rise up, mighty men,
And take your place;
Tell the lost about the Saviour
Of the human race.
Now is the time,
Do it today,
Tell everyone
That Jesus is the Way (*John 14:6*).
Put Him above
All that you cherish.
God is not willing
That anyone should perish (*2 Peter 3:9*).
Reach out and take hold of
His outstretched hand,
And stay focused on Him
As you march through the land.

Spread His love
Wherever you go,
So that the love of God
Everyone will know.
To reach every corner
Of every nation
Is the master plan
Of the God of Creation.
If each one reached one,
Very soon the job would be done.
The battle belongs to the Lord,
And has already been won
On the Cross by Jesus,
God's only Son.
Hallelujah.

Thank You, Lord.

Rest

Everyone needs a break now and then,
Whether you nurse the sick or write with your pen.
It's good to lay it all down, every once in a while,
Then you'll be restored to run that extra mile.
All of your wanderings will surely cease
When you take time out to rest
With the Prince of Peace.
Let Him hide you in the cleft of the rock,
Safe and secure from the things that shock.
Listen to Him as He sings you a song,
Cradled in His arms where you belong.
Rest awhile under the shadow
Of the Almighty's wings,
And you'll be restored and renewed
By the King of Kings.
For some to rest is quite a test,
But when we're running low on zest,
God's filling station is the best.
Plug into the pump, that is called refill,
Then, as you wait on the Lord to fill you,
Just be still.
You'll soon be so full that you'll overflow,
Then you can give what He's given
To those who are running on low.
If you hold back what is meant to flow,
It will stagnate within and have nowhere to go.
The blockage will cause
Suffering and pain in your heart,
But there is a way
For it to depart.
Ask God to turn
The stop valve to release,
Then the dam will burst forth,
Bringing great joy and peace.
Hallelujah.

Thank You, Lord.

The King of Kings

When the night is cold,
You are there.
When darkness surrounds me,
You hear my prayer.
Though You are the King
Who sits on the throne,
You promised that You'd never
Leave me alone.
You are
Faithful and true,
And I can do nothing
Without You.
You are my hope
When all else fails.
Lord, You are the wind
In my sails.
When my head is bowed low
And my energy is spent,
It's You who straightens me up
When my back is bent.
When I call out,
You hear my cry.
You are the One who lifts
My head up high.
I once was lost,
But now I am found.
You untied the shackles
That held me bound.
Your death on the Cross
Set me free,
To become the woman that God
Intended me to be.
With You, Lord,
I can do all things.
You are my Lord and Saviour,
The King of all Kings.
Hallelujah.

Thank You, Lord.

From Defection to Perfection

The Lord has taken off
My filthy rags,
And He is stripping me daily
Of my sinful tags.
He loved me even when
I was so unclean,
And one day I'll be cleaner
Than I've ever been.
He came to rescue me
From the devil's snare,
So that I could live
Without a care.
What began in perfection,
Ended in defection,
But my heavenly Father showed me love,
And not rejection.
He came down to earth
From heaven above,
To show the world
The full extent of His love.
"For God so loved the world
That He gave His only begotten Son,
That whoever believes in Him
Should not perish,
But have everlasting life" (*John 3:16*).
We are being changed
From defection to perfection,
From glory to glory,
By the power of the resurrection.
Jesus said, "I am the Resurrection and the Life.
He who believes in Me,
Though he were dead,
Yet he shall live" (*John 11:25*).

Thank You, Lord.

Die to Self

We must continue to nourish
Whatever we sow.
If a seedling didn't get fed and watered,
It would not grow.
Once it's been planted,
We can no longer see it with our eye,
And before that seed can multiply,
First it has to die.
Change brought that little seed
Much trouble and strife,
But it had to die to self
To bring forth new life.
It was willing to die
For many others.
Now it has a multitude
Of sisters and brothers.
Sow a seed and grow a crop,
Then nurture it well, so that none will drop.
When we plant seeds into the right ground,
One day an abundant harvest will be found.
Seeds are so precious,
Handle them with care,
Go forth and plant them, here, there and everywhere.
Sow the seeds only in good soil, so that none will spoil.
What the Lord has prepared will spare you much toil.
From the seeds that the Lord of the harvest
Gave you to sow,
An abundant harvest will surely grow.
When you have more than enough to spare,
Remember to give, for it is good to share.
Whatever you give away,
Will always come back –
More than enough
To overflow your sack.

Thank You, Lord.

When I Met You

Before I met You
I had no one to tell my problems to.
When I woke up in the middle of the night,
No one was there to hold me tight.
Before I met You
I had to face many fears on my own.
There was no one to comfort me
When I was lost and alone.
Before I met You
I often prayed for a better life,
And for someone to rescue me
From all my strife.
Then I met You.
Your love overwhelmed me
And healed my mind.
You are awesome and wonderful,
Gentle and kind.
When I met You,
You lifted me out of
The miry clay,
And I love You more and more
With each passing day.
You alone are faithful and true –
Where would I be if I hadn't met You?
Today I am no longer on my own,
You promised that You'd never
Leave me alone.

I love You, Lord, with all my heart.
Thank You for giving me
A brand-new start.
One day at a time
Is how You want me to walk,
And I will guard well
The talk that I talk.
I will love others
The way You love me,
And I'll remember the Cross where You died
To set me free.
There is nothing or no one
That I love more than You,
And I know, without a doubt,
That You love me too.
Hallelujah.

Thank You, Lord.

Sustain Your Focus

Life is too short to be little,
So it is good to have some fun.
Remember to be sincere but not too serious
In your daily run.
Whatever you stay focused on,
You are sure to get,
So you should always be specific
With the goals that you set.
"Whatever the mind of man
Can conceive and believe,
He will receive."
But if you have broken focus,
You will soon realise
That at the end of the path you walked on
There won't be any prize.
Focus on the possibility,
And not on the limitation,
Then walk out in faith,
And reach the nation.
If you get off the train
At the wrong station,
You will never reach your destination.
Keep on going
At a steady pace.
Sustain your focus
And you will win the race.

Thank You, Lord.

Do Not Lose Heart

Is your cup nearly empty?
Are you needing a fresh drink?
Are your dreams lying broken?
Are you on the brink?
Has your light gone out?
Have you lost your shine?
Have you forgotten what it feels like
To be doing fine?
Have you almost come to
The end of your rope?
Well, hold on a minute,
I want to tell you there's hope.
There's a winner inside every one of us,
Have no doubt,
But we need to open up the door
And let him out.
People will try to hold you back,
There will always be some,
But no one can hold back the man
Whose time has come.
Never, never, never give up.
Come and take a drink
From the winner's cup.
He'll fill you so full that you'll overflow,
Then you can pass it on to others
Wherever you go.
Galatians 6 verses 9 and 10 says,
"Let us not grow weary,
While doing good,
For in due season we shall reap,
If we do not lose heart."
And there's no better time than now
To make a new start.

Thank You, Lord.

The Dream

Are you chugging along like a car
That's running low on fuel?
Do you feel like you're in the middle of
A really hard duel?
Does everything seem to be going wrong,
With nothing going right?
Are you feeling right now
Like giving up the fight?
You must do something before
You reach the end of your rope.
Relight the fire in your heart
And you'll rekindle lost hope.
The dream is the fuel that you need
To reignite your fire,
And it will propel you along
To reach your heart's desire.
The dream will help you to overcome
All the problems that mount,
And if your dream is big enough,
The facts won't count.
"Hope deferred makes the heart sick" (*Proverbs 13:12*),
But achieving your dream makes you healthy,
So don't delay, do it quick.
Relight your fire,
That's now a tiny peep,
And awaken those dreams
That have fallen asleep.

Thank You, Lord.